Glowing Life Public

30 AMAZING VEGAN

SALAD

DRESSING

RECIPES

INSANELY DELICIOUS, HEALTHY, RAW, GLUTEN-FREE DRESSINGS THAT ARE EASY-TO-MAKE IN LESS THAN 5 MIN

(YOU DON'T HAVE TO BE VEGAN TO LOVE THESE)

Copyright © 2022 by Glowing Life Publications

Glowing Life Publications has no responsibility for the persistence or accuracy of URLs for external or third-party Internet Websites referred to in this publication and does not guarantee that any content on such Websites is, or will remain, accurate or appropriate.

Designations used by companies to distinguish their products are often claimed as trademarks. All brand names and product names used in this book and on its cover are trade names, service marks, trademarks and registered trademarks of their respective owners. The publishers and the book are not associated with any product or vendor mentioned in this book. None of the companies referenced within the book have endorsed the book.

Disclaimer: Your health is your responsibility. None of the recommendations or information contained in this publication should be considered medical advice. The publisher and distributors of this media recommend that you consult a physician / health professional before making any dietary change or implementing a new exercise program. While every attempt has been made to verify the information provided in this e-book, neither the author nor his affiliates and partners are responsible for errors, inaccuracies or omissions. The responsibility for any consequences resulting from any suggestion or procedure described hereafter does not lie with the author, publisher or distributors of this book.

First edition

ISBN-13: 979-8-821162-48-9

www.glowinglife.net

"Your health is what you make of it.
Everything you do and think
either adds
to the vitality, energy and spirit
you possess
or
takes away from it."

Ann Wigmore

Contents

Introduction

Having good salad dressings that you love is one of the KEYS to success in a healthy diet. Many people are not interested in eating salads, because if they order one in a restaurant, it will be usually a small heap of some lettuce leaves (that comes sometimes wilted from a pre-washed and pre-cut plastic bag), three slices of tomatoes and some grated carrots. Overall something not very substantial and a "meal" that leaves you hungry after. The dressing is often just oil and vinegar or some ready-made sauce from the supermarket containing questionable ingredients that don't benefit your body, if not even harming you (preservatives, artificial flavors, etc.). Therefore, to most people salad means boring food and not satisfying. But this recipe book will open a new world of tasty, satisfying AND healthy salads for you and it will hopefully change your mind how you think of salads in future.

Some of these recipes you can also turn easily into a dip by reducing the added water. We also have written the minimum amount of salt in the ingredients lists, because we believe that less salt is more beneficial for your body, because there is now salt in almost all foods that you can buy in restaurants or supermarkets and therefore you can quickly exceed the daily recommended intake. Feel free to add a pinch more if you prefer a saltier taste.

All recipes in this book are gluten free. Not all ingredients are raw, but you can omit these or use a raw version of it.

Salads are far from boring...

...if you know some little tricks how to prepare them. With a good salad dressing you can make any vegetables in your salads just taste great. And most dressings will take less than 5 minutes to prepare with the help of a good blender. We have developed dozens of amazing salad dressings for our online

Glow & Grow Academy program, so you will never get bored of eating salads. And we keep adding new, proven recipes into our academy video database.

No more boring salads!

To keep the price of the book low for you we decided not to include colored images in this paperback book. There will be a premium hardcover book coming soon with images, but not everyone is willing to pay a high price for salad dressings and therefore we wanted to make an affordable offer that no one stops from starting a new, delicious salad life because of the price. Salad dressings are also so easy to make so images how it will look will not assist a great deal in achieving impressive results. You can find however images and more recipes on our website, Instagram and Facebook pages:

Website: www.glowinglife.net
Instagram: www.instagram.com/RawVeganArt/
Facebook: www.facebook.com/RawVeganCulinaryArt/

To receive more recipes, tips and techniques for making your life healthier and more glowing, join our free monthly Glowing Life newsletter. Don't worry we won't spam you and you can cancel it any time you want.

Don't skip the salt free salad dressing chapter if you are not interested in a salt free diet. You can still get amazing dressing recipes here and of course you are free to add a pinch of sea salt. We created this chapter, because I know there are many raw vegan people out there who avoid salt. Not all dressing recipes will be mind-blowing, but we know the recipes in the salt free chapter will work perfectly fine without any salt.

The ingredients lists are written in order more or less in which we recommend to put the ingredients in your blender. It helps to achieve the right flavors and textures if you pay attention to the order in which you fill your blender, because for example seeds should be always at the bottom so they will be blended more than the ingredients added on the top. Salt and small seeds should also be at the bottom of the container otherwise it will end up on the sides and you have to scrape it down.

Spices and herbs should come ideally after you finished with the high speed blending, because if you blend spices on high speed you will lose a lot of flavor. So we blend in the spices at lower speed once we finished high speed blending the base ingredients. Fresh garlic we blend on high speed which will reduce the potency, but will keep the garlic flavor.

If you use a personal blender where you can't blend on a low speed, we recommend to cut the herbs finely with a sharp knife and then stir it into the dressing without blending it. The high speed blending will destroy some of the aromatic flavors of the herbs which we want to preserve in our dressings.

Tools, Staple Foods & Preparation

What Tools Do I Need To Make My Dressings?

It is so beneficial for your beautiful body when you prepare your dressing from raw ingredients, because they will contain more enzymes and bio photons that would be destroyed when heating or pasteurizing your dressings.

To achieve a creamy texture, we highly recommend to get a good high-speed blender, such as the Vitamix. There are many cheaper alternatives available now, some cost even less than 100 $ and come with a large and small container. The important thing is that the engine is strong and fast. The blender should have a speed of minimum 25000 RPM.

Check our website www.glowinglife.net for recommendations.

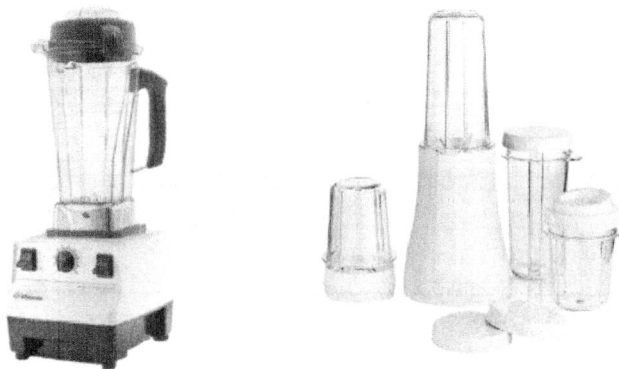

When using small quantities, the blending won't work very well in the large container of the Vitamix and therefore we recommend also a small NutriBullet / Personal Blender with a small container. The smaller personal blender is also perfect for grinding fresh coffee beans, flax and chia seeds. This one is also easier to take with you when you travel.

Prepare Your Nuts And Seeds

Soaking of nuts and seeds is more important than you might think. Nuts and seeds contain enzyme inhibitors to protect them, but these also disturb our digestion and therefore absorption of nutrients. Soaking nuts and seeds will reduce or even neutralize the enzyme inhibitor, which makes them more digestible. It requires to think a little bit ahead of your meal preparation, but you can just soak small quantities that will be used for sure within the next 2 days. When you go the extra mile of soaking your nuts and seeds you will not just get a creamier texture of your dressings, but also you will be able to digest them better and increase the nutrients in your dressings, because the germination process will unlock more vitamins and beneficial enzymes.

Soaked almonds are always a good snack. Whenever you want to snack something you can just go to your fridge and get a few of soaked almonds. You don't feel so thirsty after eating some soaked almonds which you normally would when eating dried almonds. But don't worry, if you don't want to go through the joy of the soaking process, you can always replace the soaked almond in the following recipes by using 1-2 tablespoons of almond butter. Almond butter has a long shelf life so you can buy a large jar which is cheaper.

Cashews are softer and don't require long soaking hours to achieve a creamy texture in a Vitamix blender. If you forgot to soak some almonds last night you can use a few cashew nuts instead. Wash them to remove any dust and traces of mold and place them first in your large blender container. We still recommend to soak them for at least 2 hours especially if you use a personal blender, because the personal blender will not produce a super smooth texture when they are still dry. Soaking will also make them more digestible.

Always rise your nuts before use to remove any dirt and traces of mold.

Do We Have A Date? – Natural Sweetener

There are many varieties of dates available, but I usually only buy the Medjool dates. They are more expensive, but they are also larger, softer and sweeter. They have a nice caramel flavor which most other type of dates don't have, so they are perfect for any chocolate dishes and desserts. Alternatively, you can buy Mazafati or Kabkaab dates. Check your local oriental store and organic supermarkets.

The most sold type of date is however the Deglet Noor, which are smaller, cheaper and also less impressive in flavors than the Medjool type. They are also harder and therefore you need to soak them overnight if you want to use them in a dressing or a smoothie, otherwise you will have big chunks left - even in a Vitamix blender. To achieve the right sweetness of your food you might need 2-3 Deglet Noor instead of only 1 Medjool. At the end you will probably pay nearly the same price as for the Medjool dates, because you need to use more the Deglet Noor. Furthermore, you will not get a wow flavor in your food.

We usually remove the seeds of 3 dates and put them in a small jar, add a little bit of filtered water and store them in a fridge. These last a couple of days whenever to make a nice smoothie, ice cream or salad dressings. Once you used them up you can also blend the sweet soaking water in one of your salad dressings. Wash the jar and refill it with new dates and water.

Other sweetener alternatives to sugar are:

- coconut blossom sugar (not raw)
- honey (raw, but not vegan)
- agave syrup (not healthy, because high in fructose [1])
- apple syrup (available in raw quality)
- maple syrup (not raw)
- stevia leaves (make tea and use the stevia tea instead of water)
- yacon syrup (available in raw quality)
- monk fruit syrup
- rice syrup (not raw)
- raisins

So Many Soy Sauces

There are many soy sauces available on the market and we recommend to get a really good soy sauce that has been traditionally brewed, because the normal sauces in the supermarkets are usually not produced in a traditional way. Chances are high that you get a sauce that has been colored with brown coloring and is loaded with salt and you get stomach pain after using it. And yes, don't get Kikkoman because they are using genetically modified organisms to brew the sauce in 3 months instead of 2 years. Traditionally brewed soy sauces ripen slowly in wooden barrels for 2 years and you are most likely to find them in an organic market. Organic soy sauces are also not made from genetically modified soy beans. Check the label on the bottle if it tells you how long it was fermented. A good soy sauce you can keep for years in your refrigerator. It will continue to ferment and when you open it, it will pop a bit. Over time it also gets thicker.

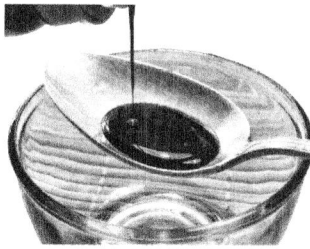

If you want to avoid gluten in your diet buy an organic tamari sauce which is made from soy beans only. The cheaper shoyu sauce is made from wheat and soybeans. Nama Shoyu isn't technically a raw soy sauce raw because the ingredients (soy and wheat) where heated before fermentation, but when finished it is not being pasteurized. It is not gluten-free either.

Other alternatives are Bragg Liquid Aminos (gluten-free) and Coconut Aminos (gluten-free).

No More Boring Salads

In this chapter we have gourmet level salad dressing recipes and focus on the enjoyable taste of a salad dressing, disregard if we need nuts, oil or salt. These recipes are to impress your friends and family or just to treat yourself.

Tomato Sauce Dressing

Ingredients:
1 small fresh tomato, quartered
6-8 of soaked sun-dried tomatoes (depending the size)
Pinch of sea salt to taste (optional - depends how salty your sun-dried tomatoes are)
1 celery stalks without the leaves, roughly chopped
1/2 cup zucchini, roughly chopped
1/2 avocado (alternatively: 2 tablespoons of olive oil)
4 tablespoon of filtered water
1 teaspoon lemon juice or apple cider vinegar
a bit of fresh dill and parsley (alternatively basil, rosemary and oregano go very well in here, too)

Directions:
Blend all ingredients except the herbs in a personal blender until smooth. If it is too thick you can add a bit more water or another fresh tomato. Chop the fresh herbs finely and add them to the sauce. Do not blend them in the blender. You may not need to add sea salt, because often the sun-dried tomatoes are salty enough. Try first without adding salt, you can still add a pinch later. If you don't want any bitter flavor, make sure no lemon seed will drop into the sauce before blending.

Serving Suggestion:
You can serve this salad dressing with zucchini noodles, chopped lettuce, cucumber, red peppers, radicchio, finely shaved cabbage. Add 1-2 chopped sun-dried tomatoes. Sprinkle with some pumpkin or sunflower seeds.

Creamy Orange Dressing

Ingredients:
20 almonds, soaked 8 hours
¼ teaspoon sea salt
¼ teaspoon mustard seeds
1 teaspoon of cold pressed oil
1 sweet orange, peeled
½ peeled lemon
1 Medjool date, soaked
3 mint leaves (alternatively basil)
1 cup of filtered water

Directions:
Cut the orange in half and remove all seeds (they will turn the dressing bitter if you miss one). Also remove the seeds from the lemon half. Put the almonds first in the blender, then add salt, oil, mustard seeds and a soaked and pitted date. Fill in a cup of water, close the lid and blend everything on high speed until it is creamy. Then add the mint or basil leaves (not both, only one type depending what you have) and blend them in on low speed.

Serving Suggestion:
This dressing goes very well with grated carrot-apple salad, fennel, shredded cabbage or a Coleslaw type of salad.

Raw Ranch Dressing

Ingredients:
1¼ cup of cashews, soaked for at least 2 hours
1 clove of garlic
¼ cup lemon juice
1 cup of filtered water
3 tablespoons apple cider vinegar
2 tablespoons of olive oil
½ Medjool date, soaked
2 inch (= 5 cm) the white end of a spring onion
1 tablespoon nutritional yeast (optional)
½ teaspoon sea salt
Freshly ground pepper
3 tablespoon of chives, finely chopped
3 tablespoon of dill, finely chopped

Directions:
Strain the soaked cashews and rinse them. Put everything in the order above in your high-speed blender except the ground pepper. Blend everything on high speed, add the ground pepper, finely chopped chives and blend for 1-3 seconds on low speed.

Serving Suggestion:
A wonderful creamy dressing for all types of lettuce with tomatoes, cucumber, savoy cabbage, kale and radishes.

Thousand Island Dressing

Ingredients:
5 sun-dried tomatoes, soaked in a little bit of water for 20 minutes if too dry
1 cup of cashew nuts, soaked for minimum 2 hours
1 ripe, sweet orange, peeled
Juice of a small lemon
2 cups of filtered water
1 Medjool date, soaked
1 clove of garlic
2 tablespoon apple cider vinegar
2 tablespoons cold-pressed sunflower or canola oil
2 tablespoons of tamari or Nama Shoyu
¼ sweet, red bell pepper

Directions:
When you have really dry sun-dried tomatoes it is better to soak them in water for about 20 minutes. If you have the soft, oily sun-dried tomatoes you don't need to soak them. Place them in your high-speed blender. Drain the cashews and rinse them. Place them as well in your blender container. Squeeze the lemon in a lemon press and add the juice without any seed into your blender container. Peel the orange, quarter it and remove the seeds as well. Add all the other ingredients from the list above and blend on high speed. When smooth you can add freshly ground pepper and 3 tablespoons finely chopped parsley. Do not blend the herbs and peppers on high speed, just on lowest speed for a few seconds.

Serving Suggestion:
Once you have made this you never want to buy this dressing anymore from the supermarket. It goes very well with any type of lettuce, radish, carrots, cabbages, broccoli, apples, fennel, bell peppers, cucumbers and tomatoes.

Spicy Almond dressing

Ingredients:
2 tablespoons almond butter (alternatively ½ cup of soaked almonds)
3 egg tomatoes
Generous fingernail piece of ginger
1 tablespoons nama shoyu
1 tablespoons of maple syrup
1 teaspoon miso
Lime juice of 1 lime
1 inch (= 2 cm) of fresh lemon grass
1 small chili (add more later if you like it spicy)
2 tablespoons of filtered water

Directions:
Wash the ginger under hot water. When you use hot water, the ginger will be less bitter. You can peel the ginger, but you can also keep the peel. Chop the tomatoes in quarters. Remove the hard outer leaves from the lemon grass (you can juice them or make tea from them) and use the softer parts of the lower end. Blend all ingredients in a high speed blender until completely smooth. Start with 1 chili and then try if you want to have it spicier. One chili might be enough.

Serving Suggestion:
This dressing goes well on lettuce, kale and shredded cabbage with carrots.

Creamy Pumpkin Seeds Dressing

Ingredients:
¼ cup of pumpkin seeds, preferably soaked about 8 hours or more
1 clove of garlic
1 teaspoon of miso
¼ teaspoon of sea salt
¼ teaspoon of sweet paprika powder
1 Medjool date, preferably soaked
1 tablespoon of apple cider vinegar
1 tablespoon of pumpkin seed oil
½ zucchini, roughly chopped
Juice of ½ of a small lemon
5 tablespoons of filtered water
2 basil stalks

Directions:
Place all the ingredients in your high-speed blender except the basil and blend it on high speed until smooth. Add the basil stalks and maybe a bit more water if needed and blend again on low speed.

Serving Suggestion:
This wonderful dressing goes very well on raw broccoli, tomatoes, cabbages, sprouts, fresh sweet peas, and lettuces.

Open Sesame Dressing

Kala Namak – also known as "Himalayan black salt" – is a rock salt from northern India, that has been heated in a furnace for hours together with some plants and has a sulfuric, pungent smell. You can use it to create meals that will taste like cooked egg (scrambled tofu for example). We know it is a little bit difficult to find, but it is really worth to search for this salt in a health food store near you.

Ingredients:
1 Medjool date, soaked
1 inch (2 cm) of leek
1 large tablespoon of tahini
¼ teaspoon of Kala Namak salt (don't worry – if you don't have this you can use sea salt or 1 teaspoon of miso as well)
1 large tomato, roughly chopped
1 slice of lemon, chopped in half
1 tablespoon of apple cider vinegar
1 tablespoon of sunflower oil or olive oil
1 stalk of basil

Directions:
Brush the lemon under hot water, this will make the lemon peel (which we are going to use) less bitter. Cut the lemon in half and cut off a slice from the middle. Remove the green part of the tomato and place all the ingredients (except the fresh basil) in order of the list into your high speed blender. Remove the lower hard part of the basil stalk. If the stalk is soft, you can use it all. Add the basil into your blender and blend on low speed shortly (1-3 second, depending on your blender).

Serving Suggestion:
This special dressing goes well on shredded fennel, cabbages, lettuce, cucumbers, bell peppers and sprouts.

Coriander Pesto Dressing

Coriander greens promotes healthy eye-sight, manages diabetes symptoms and is being used for heavy metal detoxification. If you are new to it, we recommend not to use too much at the beginning.

Ingredients:
2 cloves of garlic
½ zucchini / courgette
¼ teaspoon sea salt or herbal salt
½ large avocado or 1 whole small avocado
1 tablespoon olive oil
Juice of ½ of a lemon or 1 whole lime
2 tablespoons of filtered water
1 bunch of coriander (approximately ¾ cup)
3 tablespoon soaked almonds, alternatively sunflower seeds or pumpkin seeds
Freshly ground pepper / optional: 1 tablespoon nutritional yeast

Directions:
Blend everything except the last three ingredients in your high-speed blender until creamy. Then add the soaked almonds, and the finely chopped coriander and blend everything shortly on low-medium speed. There should stay some almond chunks in the pesto. If you want to imitate some of the typical parmesan flavor in this dressing you can add 1 tablespoon of nutritional yeast.

Serving Suggestion:
This recipe will go very well on tomatoes, cucumbers, fennel, peppers or zucchini noodles.

Creamy Coriander Dressing

Coriander greens promotes healthy eye-sight, manages diabetes symptoms and is being used for heavy metal detoxification. If you are new to it, we recommend not to use too much at the beginning.

Ingredients:
1 medium garlic clove
12 soaked almonds (alternative: 1 tablespoon almond butter)
12 cashew nuts (preferably soaked for 2 hours, but it will work without soaking)
2 tablespoons of sunflower oil or canola oil
½ teaspoon of mustard seeds
½ zucchini / courgette
Juice of 1 lime (alternatively: juice of ½ a lemon)
3 tablespoons of filtered water
¼ teaspoon sea salt
½ dried chili
Freshly ground pepper
½ bunch of coriander / cilantro, chopped finely

Directions:
Wash the coriander green. Peel the garlic clove. Place everything (except the ground pepper and coriander) as in the order above in your high speed blender container and blend on high speed until creamy. Add the freshly ground pepper and the chopped coriander into the mixture and blend again shortly (1-3 second) on low speed.

Serving Suggestion:
This dressing goes very well on finely shredded red cabbage with some ginger and oranges. Any leafy greens, tomatoes, red peppers as well.

Brazil Pepper Dressing

This recipe is not so suitable for the small personal blenders, because you will have a grainy consistency from the brazil nuts. But you might like it a bit chunky and crunchy.

Ingredients:
1 large red pepper (about 2 cups)
½ teaspoon of sea salt
12 brazil nuts (preferably soaked over night)
A fingernail size of fresh turmeric (about 1 inch / 2 cm)
A fingernail size of fresh ginger (about 1 inch / 2 cm)
1 clove of garlic
½ fresh, red chili (depends how spicy you like it) – alternatively, a bit of a dried chili pepper
2 tablespoons of lemon juice
¼ cup of filtered water
1 ½ teaspoon of sweet curry powder (not a spicy curry powder)

Directions:
Wash the ginger under hot water. When you use hot water, the ginger will be less bitter. Blend everything in your high-speed blender except the curry powder until it is smooth. Then add the curry powder and blend shortly (1-3 seconds) on low speed.

Serving Suggestion:
This dressing will go very well on tomato salads, cucumber, leafy greens and lettuce.

Creamy Pear Dressing

This recipe works well in autumn or whenever in your area pears are in season. Out of season we do not recommend to buy pears because they are too hard and lack of sweetness and flavor.

Ingredients:
12 almonds, soaked 8 hours
1 tablespoon of flax seeds
¼ teaspoon of sea salt or herbal salt
1 clove of garlic
4 whole fennel seeds
1 fingernail size of ginger
2 large, ripe pears, chopped
1 tablespoon of apple cider vinegar
2 tablespoons of water

Directions:
Wash the ginger under hot water. When you use hot water, the ginger will be less bitter. You don't need to peel the ginger, but when you remove the peel, it will be also less bitter. Blend everything in your high-speed blender with little water so that it stays creamy.

Serving Suggestion:
This will go very well on endive / chicory, fennel or any soft type of cabbage (sweetheart cabbage, napa / Chinese cabbage, green cabbage with some grated carrots) as well and leafy greens.

Creamy Orange Dressing

Kala Namak – also known as "Himalayan black salt" – is a rock salt from northern India, that has been heated in a furnace for hours together with some plants and has a sulfuric, pungent smell. You can use it to create meals that will taste like cooked egg (scrambled tofu for example). We know it is a little bit difficult to find, but it is really worth to search for this salt in a health food store near you.

Ingredients:
2 tablespoons of almond butter
Juice of ½ a lemon, seeds removed
1 small orange, peeled
½ cup filtered water
4 tablespoons of sunflower seed or canola oil

Directions:
Blend all the ingredients in a blender with a small container. Then add the following ingredients and blend everything for 1-2 seconds again:

2 tablespoons of tamari or nama shoyu
1 pinch of freshly ground nutmeg
1 tablespoon of dried or fresh oregano / marjoram
1 tablespoon of rosemary leaves
¼ teaspoon of Kala Namak salt (don't worry – if you don't have this you can use sea salt or 1/2 teaspoon of miso as well)

Serving Suggestion:
A beautiful dressing for 2 large salads for 2 people of lettuce, turnips, fennel, or shredding pumpkin. Also beetroot, carrot + apple combos work well with this dressing.

Zucchini Dill Dressing

Dill contains essential oils that supports good sleep. Dill is rich in calcium which fortifies bone health.

Ingredients:
1 medium Zucchini, roughly chopped
20 soaked almonds (alternatively 2 tablespoons of almond butter)
½ cup of filtered water
1 tablespoon of sesame or sunflower oil
1 tablespoon tamari or nama shoyu
¼ bunch of dill

Directions:
Place everything in your high-speed blender container in the order above, except the dill. Blend everything until creamy. Chop the Dill finely and add it to the mixture. Blend everything again for 1-2 seconds on low speed.

Serving Suggestion:
A quick, creamy dressing that works on all vegetables: shredded cabbage with grated apple, raw cauliflower, grated carrots, lettuce, cucumbers, bell peppers, radishes, spinach and oranges, Swiss chard and turnips.

Walnut Dressing

We really recommend to soak the walnuts for 4-8 hours or longer, because they are easier to digest after soaking and also less bitter. Discard the soaking water.

Ingredients:
1 clove of garlic
Juice of ½ lemon
½ apple, peeled
3/4 cup walnuts, soaked
½ cup of filtered water
½ zucchini, roughly chopped
1 cup of water
1 teaspoon paprika powder
1 teaspoon dried oregano
¼ teaspoon ground cumin
1 teaspoon miso

Directions:
Wash the apple, cut it in half and remove the flower part and core. You can blend it including the core, but the apple seeds might make the dressing more bitter than what you like. But the flower and stem part should be cut off, because they are usually still a bit dirty after washing. Strain the walnuts, pour away the soaking water and rinse them in a strainer. Place all the ingredients in your high-speed blender and puree everything on high speed until you reach a smooth consistency. Then add the spices and miso and blend again for a few seconds on low speed.

Serving Suggestion:
This goes very well on everything, from carrots, beet roots, sunchoke, lettuce, tomatoes, cucumbers, cabbages, raw broccoli, spring onions and radishes.

Nut-Free Salad Dressings

Why Nut-Free Salad Dressings

Nuts are high in protein and fats, which can be a problem for sensitive people. Some people have allergies against nuts. You can do a kinesiology test (= muscle test) to see if your body accepts them. The result of the test can be different if you use dry or soaked/activated nuts. If you have skin problems and eating a lot of nuts, it might be worth to abstain from them for a while to see if this will improve the condition.
Nutmeg is a spice and it should be safe to eat on a nut-free vegan diet.

Some thoughts to be aware of:

- Nuts are high in fat and easy to over-eat
- If you had to crack every nut yourself, how many would you eat then? Since they are already cracked for us, it is easy to eat more than what our body can digest.
- Nuts are often moldy or rancid without showing signs. Therefore, wash always your nuts before you consume them. Brazil nuts often taste moldy and walnuts often taste rancid.
- When you buy nuts they could be already one year old.

We recommend to soak your nuts before consuming which makes them more digestible. Instead of nuts we recommend to use more sprouts, sprouted quinoa and buckwheat instead of nuts. Tiger nuts (chufas) are also an alternative, but they tend to get moldy quickly as well.

Here are now our nut free dressing recipes. However, some recipes contain seeds which are a bit easier to digest than nuts, especially when soaked and activated.

Ginger-Miso Dressing

Ingredients:
1 tablespoon of white/yellow miso
1 soft Medjool date, preferably soaked
3 tablespoon of apple cider vinegar
¼ cup of cold pressed sesame oil (alternatively any other oil)
¼ cup lemon juice (seeds removed)
¼ cup ginger, chopped

Directions:
Wash the ginger under hot water. When you use hot water, the ginger will be less bitter. For this recipe we recommend to cut off the peel of the ginger. Chop the ginger finely.

For this recipe you would need a small blender container, such as the personal blender. Add all the ingredients in a small blender container and blend everything until creamy.

Serving Suggestion:
This goes very well on cucumbers, lettuce, sprouted quinoa and leafy greens with oranges or apples.

Avocado Mustard Dressing

Ingredients:
1 large avocado
1 teaspoon of mustard (the spicy Dijon type of mustard, not the brown sweet one)
1 tablespoon of olive oil
2 tablespoons of filtered water
¼ teaspoon sea salt
1 stalk of basil leaves
1 pinch of freshly ground nutmeg
1 teaspoon nutritional yeast (optional)

Directions:
We know that mustard from the shop is not a raw ingredient, but we use it only in small quantity and with some mustard it will just taste so much better. Please buy an organic mustard since they are free of taste enhancers and preservatives. If you want to be 100 % raw you can use 1 ½ teaspoon of mustard seeds instead + 1 teaspoon of apple cider vinegar.
Scoop out the avocado and remove the seed. Wash the basil and remove hard parts of the stalk, soft parts you can use. Place all the ingredients in the order above (except the basil, nutmeg and nutritional yeast) in your high-speed blender container and blend until everything is smooth. Then add the rest of the ingredients and blend it again on low speed for 1-3 seconds.

Serving Suggestion:
This is really a gourmet level dressing that fits to all type of lettuces, turnips, finely shredded cabbages, tomatoes, cucumber, Swiss chard and peppers. Add diced oranges, grapefruits or apples.

Tahini-Miso Dressing

For this dressing you don't need a blender. You can prepare it with just a knife, spoon, fork and a bowl. It is mind blowing.

Ingredients:
1 ripe avocado
1 tablespoon of brown miso
2 tablespoons of tahini
Juice of ½ a lime
4 tablespoons of filtered water

Directions:
Cut the avocado in halves and remove the seed. Scoop out the avocado halves with a spoon and place them in a bowl. Mash them with a folk roughly and then add the lime juice, water, tahini and brown miso. We recommend organic chickpea miso if you can get that. Mix everything with the fork. Depending how large your avocado is you might want to add 2-3 more spoons of water, it should have a liquid consistency.

Serving Suggestion:
This is just another delicious salad dressing and comes with good probiotics from the miso paste. It goes very well on spinach, rocket / arugula, spring onions, tomatoes, cucumbers and lettuce.

Sesame-Ginger Dressing

Ingredients:
¼ cup sesame seeds, soaked over night
1 tablespoon chia seeds
1 cup of filtered water
1 Medjool date, soaked for at least 1-2 hours
Juice of 1 large lime
1 clove of garlic
1 inch (= 2 cm) ginger
4 tablespoons of cold pressed olive or sunflower oil
½ teaspoon of freshly ground cumin
1 tablespoon of white unpasteurized miso (alternatively chick pea miso)
½ bunch of chives, finely chopped

Directions:
Wash the soaked sesame seeds in a strainer and place the seeds in your high speed blender. Add the chia seeds and the soft date. Squeeze the lime juice in a lemon press and remove the seeds if there are any. You can add the seeds, but they will make the dressing bitter. Peel the ginger or wash it under hot water to reduce the bitterness. Add the other ingredients except the cumin, miso and chives. Blend everything at high speed until the sesame seeds have a smooth consistency. Add the freshly ground cumin, the miso paste and the fresh chives and blend again on low speed for a few seconds.

Serving Suggestion:
This recipe goes very well on raw cauliflower, lettuce, tomatoes, cucumbers, carrots, beet roots, sprouts and finely shredded kale or savoy cabbage.

Mustard Vinaigrette

Apple cider vinegar promotes healthy blood sugar. Dill contains essential oils that supports good sleep. Dill is rich in calcium which fortifies bone health.

Ingredients:
½ teaspoon mustard seeds
½ avocado
¼ teaspoon turmeric powder
3 tablespoons of yellow mustard
3 tablespoons of apple cider vinegar
1 Medjool date, soaked for a few hours
1 cup zucchini / courgette
½ cup of water
Pinch of sea salt
3 tablespoons finely chopped dill

Directions:
Scoop out the avocado half. Place all the ingredients except the dill in the order above into a high speed blender and blend until smooth. Pour the dressing in a bowl or jar, add the dill and mix it with a spoon. Do not blend anymore the dill since it will lose its flavor.

Serving Suggestion:
This dressing lasts for a couple of days in the refrigerator and goes well with tomatoes, cucumbers, spring onions, broccoli and lettuce.

Oil free Salad Dressings

Why Oil-Free Salad Dressings?

Fats and oil is being processed by your liver, so an oil-free diet can support your liver to heal and recover from damage. Also cooking oil such as olive or sunflower oil are not natural. You would need heavy machinery to squeeze a bit of oil out of many seeds. For one tablespoon of olive oil you would have to eat a lot of olives to get the same amount of oil which your body wouldn't accept. The fiber is also removed and when you really think of it, oil is also a very sticky liquid that won't go quickly through your body, especially when fried or heated. Try to rinse your frying pan under water after you fried something in oil. Is that oil easy to rinse off?

Furthermore, in the production of conventional cooking oil there is also heat and a chemical oil solvent being used (hexane) to extract more oil and increase the yield.[2]

Nevertheless, if you want to use some oil sparingly we recommend only to buy organic, cold pressed oils and store them in dark, cold areas. Flax seed oil goes off very quickly and will taste bitter and therefore should be used up very quickly. Alternatively, you can grind 2 spoons of flax seeds in a small blender container which will break up the walls of the seeds and help your body to get to the beneficial fats. Never pre-produce ground flax seeds for the next days, always grind fresh before use.

In many oil-free salad dressings the oils have been replaced by nuts and seeds, which are very fatty and heavy as well. If you are looking for a no nuts and no seeds dressing, check my next chapter with salt-free recipes which are delicious and free of nut and seeds. Of course you can use these and add a little bit of sea salt, miso or tamari.

But now try our oil-free recipes ideas and let us know what you think of them!

Pizza Dressing

Ingredients:
4 soft, sun-dried tomatoes
1 Medjool date, soaked for a few hours
¼ of sea salt
1 small clove of garlic (alternatively: ½ teaspoon garlic powder)
1 tablespoon of lemon juice or apple cider vinegar
2 large tomatoes, roughly chopped
1 tablespoon of dried oregano (or 2 tablespoon of fresh oregano if you have)
1 teaspoon of dried basil (or 2 stalks of fresh basil if you don't have dried basil)
3/4 teaspoon of sweet paprika powder

Directions:
Wash the fresh tomatoes and remove the green part. Place all the ingredients in the order above (except the herbs) in your high-speed blender and process until smooth. Then add the spices and blend again on low speed for 1-3 seconds. The dressing will keep for 2 days in a refrigerator.

Serving Suggestion:
Children will love this dressing. It goes very well on lettuce with bell peppers, finely chopped Chinese cabbage, baby spinach, pineapple, cucumbers, red onions and more tomatoes. Add olives for the adults.

Asian Style Tomato Dressing

Ingredients:
1 date, preferably soaked for some hours before
1 clove of garlic
2 tablespoons of whole flaxseeds (alternatively: hulled sunflower seeds)
2 medium tomatoes, roughly chopped
½ of a red bell pepper
1 large black plum or 2 small plums
1 tablespoon of apple cider vinegar
2 tablespoons of tamari or nama shoyu
1 inch (= 2 cm) piece of ginger
½ inch (1 cm) fresh galangal (alternatively: ½ teaspoon of galangal powder)
Small piece of chili depending the level of spiciness you desire

Directions:
Wash the tomatoes, the plum and the red bell pepper. One half of the red bell pepper goes into the dressing, the other into your salad. Add all the ingredients in the order above into the blending container of your high-speed blender and blend on high speed until creamy.

Serving Suggestion:
This is a dressing that fits to any lettuce, spinach, shredded cabbage (including finely shredded savoy cabbage), raw broccoli, tomatoes, cucumbers, zucchini / courgettes, bell peppers and carrots.

Carrot Juice Dressing

This simple dressing will taste amazing because the sulfuric flavor of the Kala Namak salt. We know it is a little bit difficult to find, but it is really worth to search for this salt in a health food store near you.

Ingredients:
1 cup of freshly squeezed carrot juice
1 generous tablespoon of almond butter
Juice of ½ a lemon (alternatively 1 orange if you don't have lemons)
½ teaspoon Kala Namak salt

Directions:
If you have a juicer make first the fresh carrot and lemon juice. If not you can buy carrot juice from a juice bar or in a bottle in supermarkets. Add a generous tablespoon of almond butter in a small blender container (NutriBullet or personal blender) as well as the carrot juice, lemon juice and the salt. Blend everything until smooth.

Serving Suggestion:
This wonderful dressing goes very well on any leafy greens, lettuce, spring onions with cucumber, bell peppers and tomatoes.

Creamy Oil-Free Mustard Dressing

Ingredients:
1 teaspoon of mustard seeds
1 bay leaf, hard stem part removed
2 cups of roughly chopped zucchini / courgettes
½ ripe avocado
1 cup of water
1 cup balsamic or apple cider vinegar
¼ teaspoon sea salt or pink Himalayan salt
¼ teaspoon black pepper
1 tablespoon of fresh rosemary (alternative ½ tablespoon dried rosemary)
½ tablespoon of dried basil
1 teaspoon of dried thyme

Directions:
Place everything (except the herbs and spices) in the order above in your high-speed blender. Blend everything on high speed until smooth. Then add the pepper and herbs and blend again for 3 seconds on low speed.

Serving Suggestion:
An aromatic dressing that goes with most vegetables and some fruits: leafy greens, lettuce, tomatoes, cucumbers, some grated apples with grates beetroots, oranges and shredded cabbage, spring onion and Swiss chard.

Salt free Salad Dressings
Why salt free salads

Although salt was used to pay Roman legions once and wars were fought for it, salt is these days one of the controversial ingredients in a healthy diet. While some sources claim it is essential, others stigmatize it as being toxic. The common table salt from the supermarkets we certainly agree should be avoided, because it contains pure sodium chloride and an anti-caking agent that is certainly not beneficial for your body. Rock salt and sea salt are a natural product. They are usually free of this anti-caking agent and it has a whole bunch of other minerals. Therefore, we use rock salt (for example Himalayan salt) or sea salt in small doses in most of our salad dressing. If you are in the healing process of an ailment, you might try to eat completely salt free for a while to see if that will bring an improvement. Our salad dressing recipes will help you to still enjoy your food.

We also believe if you are using high quality, ripe organic fruits, vegetables and culinary herbs you will enjoy their natural flavors and you don't need to add a lot of salt.

Here are some of the arguments that salt critics bring up. We do not agree not disagree with them, we just want to bring your awareness to these points.

- High dietary salt results in oxidative stress and increased endothelial cell stiffness [3]
- Reducing excess dietary salt should be considered important for overall vascular health in addition to blood pressure. [3]
- Inorganic salt is poisonous and unassimilable by the human body. [4]

- Salt works as a taste enhancer and makes addictive which will cause that people eat more than what the body actually needs
- Salt improves the taste of very bland food that you wouldn't eat without salt. Try to cook noodles without salty water and eat them without a sauce. After 2 spoons you will lose interest in eating these noodles, because they taste of nothing. Therefore, salt is being used in food industry everywhere to cover up cheap ingredients that lack of flavor and minerals and it makes addictive.
- Intake of too much sodium can lead to strains on the heart and arteries and causes high blood pressure and kidney problems.
- Salt dehydrates you which means you have to drink a lot more water when you eat salty food than when you don't eat salty food.
- Salt is already in most of the processed food from bread, sauces, dips and even frozen food. If you are eating processed food and restaurant food then you might want to stop using salt when you prepare your own food, because it will lower your total intake of salt.
- Salt is a true anti-biotic (against all life, a killer). It was formerly used as an embalming agent. It is used today as a 'preservative'—killing the bacteria (life) to prevent the natural decomposition of dead organisms.[5]

Alternatives to salt are celery stalks (high in sodium) and sea weed, which is always a nice ingredient in your salads and has lots of minerals.

Now let yourself inspire from our salt free dressing recipes and let us know what you think.

Blueberry-Orange Dressing

Frozen blueberries are often sourced from the wild and have more flavor than the fresh, cultivated ones. Of course you can use fresh blueberries for this recipes, too.

Ingredients:
½ cup frozen blueberries
1 tablespoon frozen sour cherries, pitted
1 clove of garlic
1 orange, peeled
½ medium sized tomato
1 tablespoon lemon juice
2 tablespoons water
1 tablespoon apple cider vinegar
1 teaspoon dried oregano

Directions:
Add everything to your high-speed blender in the order above, except the oregano. Blend everything until everything has been liquidized. Add the oregano spice and blend on low speed shortly again.

Serving Suggestion:
This amazing dressing will go well on any leafy greens, chopped cucumbers, tomatoes, peppers, etc.

Tropical Salad Dressing

Very important: if you live in a cold country it will be difficult to get ripe and sweet mangos in a supermarket. Don't bother to use a green mango in any of your food, it is a waste of money. It is better to buy some local apples instead of an unripe mango. However, if you look in some Asian or Oriental stores, they might have soft and ripe mangos that have a great taste. Oriental shops might also have deep-frozen, fully ripe mangos. If you use a ripe mango, this recipe will just be so much yummier.

Ingredients:
1 lime, peeled
1 ripe orange, peeled
1 small ripe banana
1 small ripe mango
1 small avocado
½ bunch of fresh mint (alternatively basil or coriander / cilantro)
½ cup of coconut water (alternatively filtered water or apple juice)

Directions:
Cut the lime and the oranges in quarters and remove all of the seeds if there are any. Just one seed can make the whole dressing bitter. You can eat the seeds, they contain the whole information of a growing a large tree, but if you don't want some bitter taste it is better to remove them.
Wash the mango under hot water and give it a good brush. You can use the mango peel in this recipe. The mango peel is loaded with antioxidants and with pectin which will thicken up your dressing. Some types of mangos have a very bitter skin, in which case you might just want to use half of the skin and not all.
Place all the ingredients in your high-speed blender and blend everything shortly at high speed. You can make variations of this

dressing by changing the added herbs: mint dressing, basil dressing, dill dressing, lemon balm dressing or coriander dressing. Parsley will not go so well in this.

Serving Suggestion:
This is an awesome summer dressing that works with more fruits and vegetables: cucumbers, spinach, Swiss chard, tomatoes, pineapple, apple, orange, shredded cabbages, grated carrots or beet roots.

Mango-Orange Dressing

Here again we need a ripe, sweet mango. Don't bother if you can only find green, unripe mangos. The final result will not be impressive. You can add a date if the mango is sour, but the typical mango flavor might be missing if you use unripe mangos.

Ingredients:
1 inch (= 2 cm) vanilla bean
1 ripe mango
2 oranges, peeled and quartered
Juice of ½ lime
4 tablespoons of filtered water

Directions:
You can include a bit of the mango peel. Wash the mango under hot water and brush it well. Remove the seeds from the oranges if there any. Remove the seed from the mango and put everything into the container of your high-speed blender. Blend everything on high speed and ready is your sauce.

Serving Suggestion:
This dressing goes very well with any type of leafy greens, shredded cabbage, spinach, bell peppers, shredded carrots and tomatoes.

Strawberry Dressing

This dressing is amazing when you have local strawberries in season. We do not recommend to buy strawberries when they are not in season, because they are transported over long distances and have not much flavor. If they are not in season you can defrost frozen strawberries which usually taste way better than the fresh ones that come from a greenhouse or from far away.

Ingredients:
1 date, pitted, soaked
2 cups of strawberries
Juice from ½ a large lime (use 1 lime if they are small)
1 ripe orange, peeled
1 celery stalk, roughly chopped
½ zucchini, roughly chopped
1-2 stalks of mint or peppermint

Directions:
Remove the pit from the date and put it into your high-speed blender. Remove the greens from the strawberries and wash them well. Peel the orange, cut it in quarters and remove any seeds. If there are seeds left they might make your dressing bitter. You can eat the seeds, they are good for you, because they have stored the information of the whole new tree in it, but they give a bitter taste that not everyone likes. Juice half of a lime in a lemon press and give the juice without the seeds into your blender. Cut off the top leaves of a green celery stalk, because the leaves also have a strong taste. Wash the celery stalk well, chop the zucchini and mint and put everything into your blender. Blend everything on high speed until smooth. Add the peppermint / mint and blend again for a few seconds on medium speed.

Serving Suggestion:

This is an amazingly yummy dressing which is oil, nut and salt free. It goes very well on any arugula / rocket, baby spinach, radishes, cucumbers, tomatoes, lettuce, kale, shredded cabbages. You will love it.

Simple Dill Dressing

Dill contains essential oils that supports good sleep. Dill is rich in calcium which fortifies bone health.

Ingredients:
1 ripe orange, peeled and quartered
1 lemon, peeled and quartered
¼ teaspoon of turmeric
½ bunch of dill

Directions:
Remove the seeds from the orange and lemon. Of course you can also keep them in your dressing if you don't mind that it will taste more bitter. Blend them in a high speed blender. Add some turmeric. Wash and chop the dill roughly and add it to the mix and blend on a low speed for a few seconds.

Serving Suggestion:
This goes very well on a radish salad, beetroots, and green leaves.

Raspberry Mint dressing

Ingredients:
1 green celery stalk, roughly chopped
½ Medjool date, soaked for a few hours
1 cup of frozen or fresh raspberries
2 tablespoons of filtered water
1 stalk of mint or peppermint

Directions:
Take out the frozen raspberries if you use frozen ones and let them defrost a little bit. If you use fresh raspberries wash them. Remove the green leaves from the celery stalk (if you don't mind the bitter taste you can keep and blend them of course). Add all the ingredients except the mint/peppermint into the container of your blender and blend everything. Remove the hard parts of the mint stalks (the soft parts you can use) and add the soft parts and the leaves to the mixture. Blend for a few seconds on medium speed.

Serving Suggestion:
This light dressing will work with cucumbers, arugula / rocket, diced zucchini, tomatoes, soft cabbages finely sliced, baby spinach, apples, oranges and diced sugar melon.

Papaya Lime Dressing

Ingredients:
1 ½ cups ripe papaya
Juice of ½ a large lime (or 1 small lime)
½ Medjool date, soaked
1 green celery stalk
Pinch of chili powder
2 tablespoons of fresh thyme (alternatively 1 teaspoon dried thyme)

Directions:
Remove the papaya seeds, but keep them in a container. They are super healthy and remove certain parasites from your body. We recommend to add 2-3 tablespoons of the papaya seeds into your salad bowl. The rest you can use another day. Squeeze the lime and remove the seeds if there are any. Remove the leaves of the celery stalk if you don't like bitter flavors. Place all of the ingredients except the thyme into your high speed blender and blend everything on high speed until smooth. Add the fresh thyme and blend again on low speed for a few seconds.

Serving Suggestion:
This goes well on Chinese or savoy cabbage, lettuce, tomatoes, cucumbers, radishes, spring onions, carrots and sweet corn.

Toppings

With a few toppings you can increase the enjoyment factor of your salad a lot. They will give different textures and flavors to your meal. Here are some inspirations what you can sprinkle on the top:

- Nuts: brazil nuts, walnuts, pistachios, almonds, cashew nuts, pecans, hazel nuts, pine nuts, coconut flakes, coconut stripes
- Seeds: pumpkin seeds, sunflower seeds, hemp seeds, poppy seeds, chia seeds
- The following seeds we recommend to grind in a small personal blender container to make it easier for your body to absorb the nutrients: sesame seeds, flax seeds, sunflower seeds, chia seeds
- Chopped sun-dried tomatoes
- Edible flowers
- Sea weed flakes such as Wakame flakes, Nori flakes, Dulse flakes

- Dried fruits: raisins, sugar-free cranberries, chopped prunes, chopped sun-dried apricots or goji berries
- Finely chopped herbs: parsley, basil, chives, dill, mint, coriander / cilantro, oregano, rosemary, spring onion
- Sprouts: mung bean sprouts, alfalfa sprouts, lentil sprouts, sprouted quinoa, sprouted buckwheat, chick pea sprouts, green pea sprouts
- Fruits: blueberries, pomegranate
- Chili flakes
- Cacao nibs
- Olives
- Capers (not raw), artichokes (usually not raw)

Thank you for reading this book

We hope we could inspire you to bring your healthy diet to a higher level and that you enjoy our recipes. We would love to hear from you what you liked and what we can improve and we would be very appreciative if you left a favorable review for this book on Amazon. This would help us to grow.

You can find images and more recipes on our website, Instagram and Facebook pages:

Website: www.glowinglife.net
Instagram: www.instagram.com/RawVeganArt/
Facebook: www.facebook.com/RawVeganCulinaryArt/

We are grateful for life and sending out lots of love to you.

Resources

1) Gifford, D. (2021, August 6). Agave Syrup Is Bad For You - Small Footprint Family. Small Footprint FamilyTM. https://www.smallfootprintfamily.com/high-fructose-agave-syrup-is-bad-for-you

2) Wikipedia contributors. (2022, March 16). Cooking oil. Wikipedia. https://en.wikipedia.org/wiki/Cooking_oil

3) Edwards, D. G., & Farquhar, W. B. (2017, May 15). Vascular Effects of Dietary Salt. National Library of Medicine. https://www.ncbi.nlm.nih.gov/pmc/articles/PMC5431073/

4) POISONOUS SALTS. (n.d.). Aquarius the Water Bearer. https://web.archive.org/web/20190223205330/http://aquarius thewaterbearer.com/poisonous-salt

5) Salt. (2013, August 22). Raw Food Explained. https://www.rawfoodexplained.com/condiments/salt.html

Printed in Great Britain
by Amazon